Do You Know the Parable?

A Deeper Look Behind the Veil of Scripture

Stacey L. Mizell, Sr.

PREFACE

My purpose for writing this book was twofold: First, to teach the Word of God; and Second, to demystify Biblical scriptures that have puzzled so many for so long. My intention is for this book to act as a catalyst that ignites a burning desire within the reader to study and meditate on the Scriptures more intensely; so that he or she can rightly divide the word of Truth for himself or herself, and not be solely dependent on the revelations of others.

For it is certain that whoever applies the jewels of knowledge contained within this book will be able to create and live in a finer world.

This is the first of a series of Fig Tree Tools™ books, and I hope you find it as enlightening and energizing as I have found writing it to be!

Copyright (C) 2015 Stacey L. Mizell, Sr.

Although the author and publisher have made every effort to ensure that the information in this book was correct at press time, the author and publisher do not assume and hereby disclaim any liability to any party for any loss, damage, or disruption caused by errors or omissions, whether such errors or omissions result from negligence, accident, or any other cause. No part of this publication may be reproduced, stored in a retrieval system, or transmitted, in any form, or by any means, electronic, mechanical, photocopying, recording, or otherwise, without the prior consent of the publisher.

The Publisher makes no representations or warranties with respect to the accuracy or completeness of the contents of this book and specifically disclaims any implied warranties of merchantability or fitness for a particular purpose. Neither the publisher nor author shall be liable for any loss of profit or any commercial damages.

Printed in the United States of America.

Second Edition

Table of Contents

PREFACE II

CHAPTER ONE - *Know Thyself* 1

CHAPTER TWO - *Exodus PI (π)* 9

CHAPTER THREE - *Who Am I?* 18

CHAPTER FOUR - *Havilah: The Realm of Infinite Treasures* 28

CHAPTER FIVE - *Have You Found Him?* 44

CHAPTER SIX - *The Journey to Almondiblathaim* 54

CHAPTER SEVEN - *The Seventh Day: The Art of Silent Meditation* 67

ABOUT THE AUTHOR 81

CHAPTER ONE

Know Thyself

"Now learn a parable of the fig tree; When his branch is yet tender, and putteth forth leaves, ye know that summer is nigh: So likewise ye, when ye shall see all these things, know that it is near, even at the doors." – Matthew 24:32-33 KJV

Life

As far back as I can remember, going to church was the central theme of my existence. I spent a good part of my waking life inside the walls of my church, or in someone else's church. It may have been some church's Revival Week; Wednesday night Bible Study; Thursday night Choir Practice; Friday's Joy and Praise

Night; Saturday's Youth Night; or, a full Sunday schedule filled with Sunday School, Sunday Worship Service at 11 am, and then Sunday Evening Service at 5 pm. After years of attending these ceremonial church services, I became the walking embodiment of church. Without even reading the Bible, I knew most scriptures verbatim. From listening to some of the "old—heads" who have now passed on to glory — I still know, word for word, some of those old spiritual hymns that never made it to the hymnbooks.

Being raised in a "holy-rolling" Pentecostal church, I sometimes feel that I have seen and heard it all. I've experienced numerous visits from the fire-and-brimstone prophets, participated in those long prayer lines that endured hours, and witnessed supernatural phenomena that would make the average person feel as if he or she were in a dream. Although I was able to quote numerous scriptures precisely, and preach a congregation into a dancing frenzy, I still went through life unsure of what that "waking" world was really about. It wasn't until my latter years that I began to receive divine revelations as to the spiritual meaning behind many of the familiar Biblical scriptures. These revelations not only removed the veil covering the letters of Biblical scripture, but also unveiled the underlying meaning behind other religions, dreams, and the divine relationship between spiritual and natural phenomena. This book, as well as the other books to come in the Fig Tree Tools™ series, will explain what my experiences have taught me: that the outer world and its phenomena, even though it appears in the world without as a final reality, all started within.

The Symbolism of the Fig Tree

The word *fig* is derived from the ancient Greek word *sykon*. The word *syconium* is the modern, translated Latin version of the word *sykon*. A syconium is the type of fruit borne by figs (genus Ficus), formed by an enlarged, fleshy, hollow receptacle with multiple ovaries on the *inside* surface.

Figs, therefore, have no blossoms on their branches; for they are technically inverted flowers that store their pollen inside the fruits. The many tiny flowers produce the crunchy little edible seeds that give figs their unique texture—flowers that grow within the fruits.

Have you noticed a continual theme when discussing the fig tree? If not, then here's the heart of the matter: IT IS ALL ABOUT THE SEARCH WITHIN. The main theme of the entire Bible is the plan laid out by God for mankind to reach his salvation and freedom. The plan of salvation is finally accomplished when man fully realizes who he really is—not who the outward world says he is, but the full awareness of his spiritual identity obtained only after touching the hem of the garment of Truth within.

The Primordial Connection

"Then the word of the Lord came unto me, saying, Before I formed thee in the belly I knew thee; and before thou camest forth out of the womb I sanctified thee, and I ordained thee a prophet unto the nations."
– Jeremiah 1:4-5 KJV

The name *Jeremiah* means "one whom Jehovah sets up, forms, or establishes". The spiritually enlightened man knows that before he entered into his mother's womb, he was a formless, animating spirit waiting to become waned and waxed into some limited mortal form. The spiritually enlightened man also knows that when the defunct form dies or returns to the Earth as it originally was, the spirit of man returns back to his formless self — the spiritual being that is free of all external and outside influences. The ancient prophets and sages of old referred to this as being man's primordial state of consciousness. The primordial being within man is the spiritual entity that is always in constant and direct communication with the Creator.

The lessons contained within the Parable of the Fig Tree are the guiding light to salvation, and the mend of the gap of separation (sin) that occurred in the Garden of Eden. The lessons of the fig tree are mentioned numerous times within the Bible, but have been misinterpreted. These misinterpretations have happened for a number of reasons, but are mainly due to carnal-minded thinking.

Although I do stand on the premise that the Bible is the greatest psychological book ever written, my intent is not to disprove any person's or any group's revelations or religious insights. My goal, however, is to inspire others to not just read the Bible, but to hear (understand) the spiritual message contained within those words.

"Who also hath made us able ministers of the new testament; not of the letter, but of the spirit: for the letter killeth, but the spirit giveth life." – 2 Corinthians 3:6 KJV

Fig Tree Tool

As the fig blossoms on the inside, man's objective should be to only plant seeds (Thoughts, T) within the garden (Mind, M) that are in agreement with his innermost desires. When man remains faithful to his new state of consciousness, he is watering his garden (M) and allowing the seeds (T) to strongly take root. The hour will soon come where abiding in the new state of consciousness will bring forth a plentiful harvest of good fruit.

"Abide in me, and I in you. As the branch cannot bear fruit of itself, except it abide in the vine; no more can ye, except ye abide in me." – John 15:4 KJV

CHAPTER TWO

Exodus PI (π)

"And God said unto Moses, I AM THAT I AM: and he said, Thus shalt thou say unto the children of Israel, I AM hath sent me unto you." – Exodus 3:14 KJV

The Infinite Name of I AM

To fully understand the content of this book and others within the Fig Tree Tools Series™, allow me to first share one of my passions that led me to write this book. Not only do I have a deep love for the Bible, but I also have an affinity for mathematics. It is my belief, that if one reads the Bible closely enough, he will find mathematical patterns within the Bible that can answer many of life's most puzzling questions.

Later in my adult years, I became increasingly aware of the interconnections between the physical world and the spiritual world. I began to see and understand how mathematics could not only give insight into the laws governing the physical world, but to that of the spiritual world as well. As there will be more revelations to come in future books, here are a few Mathematical Revelations from Exodus Chapter 3:

The pair of words stated as "I AM" appears in Exodus Chapter 3 a total of six (6) times. Moreover, the pair of words stated as "AM I" appears in Exodus Chapter 3 twice (2). Therefore, with the simple addition of the forms of "I AM" within Exodus Chapter 3, we have the following:

$$(\# \text{ of "I AM"}) + (\# \text{ of "AM I"}) = 6 + 2 = 8$$

Eight is the number representing infinite new beginnings. The number "8", if rotated 90 degrees to the left or right, becomes "∞", which is the symbol representing infinity. For it is said in Hebrews 13:8, "Jesus Christ is the same yesterday, and today, and forever".

While we are discussing Hebrews, let us now consider the number of letters within the Hebrew alphabet (22). We learned early in grammar school that a group of letters forms a word; and a group of words form a sentence. Moreover, from a spiritual standpoint, frequent thought patterns will eventually crystalize into physical manifesting character as well. All thoughts and visions that are persistent in, will eventually come to pass if the visionary is steadfast in staying faithful to obtaining his or her desires.

Staying with the theme of 22 and visions, we will transition into the book of Habakkuk. Using a colon

(:) between the number "22" to form "2:2", let's read Habakkuk 2:2, and then continue reading through Verse 3:

2. "And the Lord answered me, and said, Write the vision, and make it plain upon tables, that he may run that readeth it. 3. For the vision is yet for an appointed time, but at the end it shall speak, and not lie: though it tarry, wait for it; because it will surely come, it will not tarry." – Habakkuk 2:2-3 KJV

One of man's greatest obstacles is his inability to wait and have patience; for the race is not given to the swift or to the strong, but to the one who endures to the end. All things have their uniquely appointed times to come to pass. It takes nine months for a baby to develop from conception to birth; 22 days for chicks to hatch; and three months for seasons to change. If man could just learn to trust the inner workings of the spirit, while resting in the thoughts (words) of his heart, he will soon begin to see the unraveling of his visions come to pass in his outer world. The Sabbath day, or duration of time spent in the restful assurance that one's vision is coming to pass, is represented by the number "7." While man is in this state of restful assurance, he must know that the eternal "I AM" dwelling within him and within others is faithfully bringing forth his innermost desires onto the picture screen of space and time.

Let's take the total number of letters within the Hebrew alphabet (22), and assign them the variable W.

Next, take the number 7, which represents the uniquely appointed time we must rest in the assurance that our visions will come to pass, and assign it the variable T.

When man becomes aware of his inherent, INFINITE POWER within, he is allowing his

Thought-Words (*W*) to rest in a divine duration of Time (*T*). This conclusion can be represented by the following physics equation for *Power*:

$$\text{INFINITE POWER} = (W / T) = (22 / 7) = \pi = 3.14285714286\ldots$$

For PI (π) is a number-constant that continues FOREVER AND EVER without repeating. It is the number used to calculate the circumference of a circle, which has no beginning and no end. It represents the spiritual, Infinite Being that dwells within every human being.

"Examine yourselves to see whether you are in the faith; test yourselves! Do you not realize that Christ Jesus is in you—unless, of course, you fail the test? And I trust that you will discover that we have not failed the test." – 2 Corinthians 13:5-6 NIV

Before his spiritual awakening, man is in a state of forgetfulness; he has totally forgotten who he really is. Man has therefore rendered himself powerless, by having faith in a god outside of himself. When man begins to awaken to whom he is within, he will take upon himself a greater understanding of the phrase in the Lord's Prayer that states, "Hallowed be thy Name." For the true name of the Father is "I AM"!

The Purpose

"What is the purpose of discussing the numbers 8, 22, and 7 and the symbol π? Let us recall the equation $22/7 = 3.14285714...$ (π); hence the title of this chapter, Exodus π or Exodus 3:14:

"And God said unto Moses, I AM THAT I AM: and he said, Thus shalt thou say unto the children of Israel, I AM hath sent me unto you." — Exodus 3:14 KJV

Lastly, the number 8, or infinity (∞), is illustrated by the following verse in Exodus 3:15:

"And God said moreover unto Moses, Thus shalt thou say unto the Children of Israel, the Lord God of your fathers, the God of Abraham, the God of Isaac, and the God of Jacob, hath sent me unto you: this is my name for ever, and this is my memorial unto all generations." — Exodus 3:15 KJV

Fig Tree Tool

To awaken spiritually is to know that God (I AM) truly lives within! When man begins to meditate on his Oneness with the all-encompassing Creator of the universe, and abide therein, he will realize that he and the Father of Creation are One; but his Father is greater than he is. When one abides in the secret place (within) of the Most High, all thoughts of anxiousness and worry dissipates and a peace that surpasses all understanding fills every void.

"I can of mine own self do nothing: as I hear, I judge: and my judgment is just; because I seek not mine own will, but the will of the Father which hath sent me." – John 5:30 KJV

CHAPTER THREE

Who Am I?

"And Moses said unto God, Who am I, that I should go unto Pharaoh, and that I should bring forth the children of Israel out of Egypt?" – Exodus 3:11 KJV

Life

I can vividly remember it being one late-fall, Georgia morning when I got off the school bus, that I was headed for my seventh grade homeroom. In comparison, I wasn't as cool as most of the boys my age who hung out in the halls before class. My objective, after stepping off the bus every morning, was to hurry to the classroom and attempt to kill two birds with one stone:

Do You Know the Parable?

(1) to prevent myself from being late to class; and (2) to get a head start on that day's math homework assignment, since my homeroom teacher was my math teacher as well.

How awesome was that? Either this was the greatest thing since sliced bread, or I was the early epitome of a full-fledged geek.

However, this turned out to be a bad day—and not just because I did not make it to my classroom on time to start my math homework early.

While on my way to my homeroom, my buddy, Terry Lance, stopped me in the hallway. Terry and I were very close friends; not only did we hang out together during recess time, but we also played with and shared each other's marbles. During those days, sharing marbles was the ultimate sign of friendship.

However, something happened that day that almost made me question our friendship. In a hurry to get to class, I blew past him. He shouted, "Hey!". After recognizing his voice, I turned and walked back to see what the problem was—or in our terms, "What was up?"

However, after shaking hands, he greeted me in a way that baffled me the entire day: "What's up, dog?"

Dog! "My goodness, what in Heaven's name did I do for him to call me a dog?", I wondered. Was it due to my running past him every day? Or was it due to my never having to take my math homework home?

Never the confrontational type, I held in my hurt. I went into the boy's restroom and pondered what might have I done to deserve such harsh words from my buddy. Why did he call me a dog? My name isn't dog—

it's Stacey! Even if you capitalized the "d" and made it "Dog," that still wasn't my name.

Of course, I later learned that the word "dog" or "dawg" was slang for pal, buddy, or friend. But even to this day and forever more, I still prefer to be called by my one and only true name: Stacey.

Who Am I?

Ironically, I've been guilty of something similar to Terry's greeting. My family and close friends know that I have a habit of giving anyone and everyone a nickname. There have been times when I've called a person by a certain nickname for so long, that the person will stop me and ask, "Do you even know my real name anymore?", and I'll have to sadly admit, "No." I am ashamed to even admit that a few people in my life have even said something along the lines of: "Stacey, if you don't call me by my real name, please don't call me anything at all!"

I quickly learned how sensitive people could get about their names. Whew! Testy, testy!

This is when I learned that self-identity is a powerful thing.

The Book of Exodus in the Bible is not only one of my favorite books, it's also a beautifully written story of man's initial realization of his true self. To be specific, Exodus Chapter 3 provides a striking description of man's first awakening from the waters of darkness into the marvelous light of who he truly is. Within Exodus Chapter 3, the reader, for the first time, receives the revelation of the true name of the deity we call God, Lord, Messiah, Jehovah, Yahweh, and so many other names. It is the name that rises above every other name; it is a name of majesty, infiniteness, and power. It is the name we reverence every second of the day, whether we're doing so consciously or unconsciously. It is the name that everything with breath must praise; the name that even the rocks cry out to daily.

This name is the Holy and Hallowed Name of I AM.

The I-AMness

When I speak of my personal I AM, I'm conveying the fact that I am conscious of being. The I AM is the conscious awareness of being that lives in all, and through all.

For by the I AM:

"All things were created, whether they be visible or invisible; dominions, thrones, principalities, or powers; all things were created by him and for him." — Colossians 1:16 KJV

The I AM is that formless, all-knowing, life-giving force that animates all living things. For by the I AM, we all move and possess our being. The individualized

I-AMness, if you will, within every human being is that portion of the greater I AM that allows us to move and sustain our being. The man who approaches me and says, "Hi, I am John Doe", or "Hi, I am Joe Smooth", is acknowledging a limited form of the all-knowing I AM. When man truly grasps hold to the creative power that comes from attaching any desired state to the end of "I AM", he will be given the keys to the Kingdom. However, this repentance of mind is not spoken of in mainstream religion, or in church congregations. Most religious sects feel that equating oneself with God is pretentious; a way of stealing the Lord's unique identity—perhaps even blasphemous. But, the spiritually awakened person who realizes that he is an individualized form of the greater I AM, knows that he should NOT feel as if it's a robbery or a blasphemy to set himself equal to God (the original I AM). The great instructional book of life, the Bible, has given man divine permission to do so.

Do You Know the Parable?

"Let this mind be in you, which was also in Christ Jesus: Who, being in the form of God, thought it not robbery to be equal with God: But made himself of no reputation, and took upon him the form of a servant, and was made in the likeness of men."—Philippians 2:5-7 KJV

Suppose a man, we'll call John Doe, finds himself blindfolded on a deserted island, with a sudden case of amnesia. He may not remember his race, gender, religious preference, or marital status; and when asked his name, he may have forgotten that as well. But rest assured, he will be consciously aware of being something; and whether or not he realizes it, that something is being conscious of his own I AM. The luminous heavens and the Earth can pass, but your awareness of I AM, or awareness of being, will never leave you or forsake you.

"Go ye therefore, and teach all nations, baptizing them in the name of the Father, and of the Son, and of the Holy Ghost: Teaching them to observe all things whatsoever I have commanded you: and lo, I AM with you always, even unto the end of the world."— Matthew 28:19-20 KJV

Fig Tree Tool

Buried deep within the heart of every person, resides his or her individualized I-AMness. When man becomes consciously aware of his I AM within, he gains not only a personal awareness of himself, but also a deeper connective awareness to the world without. The enlightened individual comes to realize how using God's (I AM) name in vain is to attach undesired qualities to the end of I AM. The spiritually enlightened person knows that the universe or the world without is faithful in bearing witness to him that which he feels himself to be. Because at the name of I AM, every thought must bow, in Heaven and on Earth.

Therefore, let even the weakest person say: "I AM strong."

CHAPTER FOUR

Havilah: The Realm of Infinite Treasures

"And a river went out of Eden to water the garden: and from thence it was parted, and became into four heads. The name of the first is Pishon: that is it which compassed the whole land of Havilah, where there is gold." — Genesis 2:10-11 KJV

Life

Ever since I was a child, I had repeatedly heard the old saying that goes, "It takes money to make money." But as I've progressed through life, I've come to believe in something contrary to what I had formerly accepted. I have realized that it's not money that makes money, however, it is the demand for unique ideas.

Furthermore, I prefer to use the word resources rather than the word money, because that's what money really is — a resource.

Having said that, my theory is, if all earthly resources were gathered into a single sourcing area and redistributed equally amongst all individuals, the resources would eventually be redistributed back to their former state with the passage of time. For all resources—whether in the form of persons, things or ideas—flow to whom or what will best utilize them. All resources, visible or invisible, within the universe are governed by the Laws of Supply and Demand; which brings us to the age-old question of, "Why are some people prosperous, and others not so prosperous?"

Your Greatest Gift

Every child born of a woman was conceived into sin (separation), and due to an upbringing that has taught the reliance upon the senses and the world without; we have all been shaped in iniquity. However, buried deep within the innermost parts of man's soul, resides the Ancient One of Truth. When man makes a conscious connection to this Ancient One within, and touches the hem of His garment, he will then know of the truth that shall set him free. Initially, man sets out on a fruitless journey in the world without seeking a purpose in life and happiness—only to find himself feeling robbed physically, mentally, and spiritually. He soon realizes that it has been his faithful allegiance to the world without that had been robbing him of his spiritual birthright since infancy.

"The thief cometh not, but for to steal, and to kill, and to destroy: I AM come that they might have life, and that they might have it more abundantly." – John 10:10-11 KJV

After man's spiritual awakening, he understands that he must turn inwardly and touch the garment of his own individualized I-AMness to unlock true power, wisdom and spiritual fulfillment.

Our individualized I-AMness is God's greatest gift of Himself to His Creation. Man's individualized I-AMness allows him to take a major part in the creation of his world without. Man's creative power can be likened to a movie producer to plan and coordinate the various aspects of a movie. When man has come into conscious contact with his individualized I-AMness, there are no limitations to what he can do; for his I-AMness has access to an exceedingly abundant amount of resources beyond what his natural mind can comprehend. However, the creative process of consciously writing the scripts to his new world can only begin when man fully grasps that the creative work starts within. Once possessed with this creative power, the enlightened man no longer feels the need to duplicate the efforts of others, or seek the approval of self-proclaimed gurus or sages. He knows that within the infinite storehouse of the Creative Mind lies an infinite treasure that, if utilized, will continually separate him from the masses.

"O the depth of the riches both of the wisdom and knowledge of God! How unsearchable are his judgments, and his ways past finding out!" – Romans 11:33 KJV

Man's individualized I-AMness can be likened to a service or product that is always in high demand because there are no other competitors that can supply such a good or service. Man's individualized I-AMness is literally the gift that keeps on giving; it has been given to each of us to make our marks on the world, to provide us with lifelong sustenance, and to place us before great men.

"A man's gift maketh room for him, and bringeth him before great men." – Proverbs 18:16 KJV

The River Pishon: Inflow from the Highest Intelligence

"Praise God, from Whom all blessings flow; Praise Him, all creatures here below; Praise Him above, ye heavenly host; Praise Father, Son and Holy Ghost." – "Awake, My Soul, and with the Sun," by Thomas Ken

Man, when in his unenlightened state of consciousness, does not wholeheartedly believe that within the depths of his being exists a well of infinite wisdom and understanding. This well of living water, when spiritually appropriated, will cause the seeker of truth to no longer thirst or desire fulfillment of the carnal senses from corporeal objects in the world without. For man, being born into sin and separated from the knowledge of God (I AM), initially believes that all unique ideas, suggestions, and inventions come from his diligent attention to detail and focus on worldly matters. Once man has changed (repented) from his thoughts of separation (sin), he then realizes that the kingdom of heaven is at hand (within). Once man's thoughts of separation (sin) are washed away, the enlightened man can fully apprehend that all blessings, ideas, inspirations and flashes of genius come by prayer and silent meditation on his inner I-AMness.

Genesis 2:8-11 speaks of a garden planted eastward in Eden. Coming out of Eden flowed a river to water the garden, and the river was parted into four heads. The first of these parted riverheads is the Pishon.

When man awakens to the spiritual and mental aspects of the Bible, he will come to realize that the Bible is the greatest psychological book ever written. For the Bible is the instructional book explaining, in detail, the interwoven workings of mind, body, and spirit. Eden is that state of consciousness where all manner of ideas reside. It is that realm of infinite substance from which all blessings flow; where God or

Creative Mind rests, and where mankind is in direct contact with God (I AM).

Eden is representative of the region of God or Creative Mind that contains within it the infinite storehouse of all the primordial ideas that are readily available to man for the manifestation of his desire. Man, being made in the image of God or Creative Mind, is a miniature form of the greater I AM, and gets his inflow of ideas from the greater fountainhead of Eden. The river Pishon represents the region within the mind of man that receives its source of ideas and intelligence from the greater Creative Mind.

Opening the Floodgates of Eden

"For the wages of sin is death, but the gift of God is eternal life through Jesus Christ our Lord." – Romans 6:23 KJV

As every individual is born into sin (separation), he or she is initially separated from the knowledge of God

(I AM) and therefore lacks understanding of how to reestablish that fundamental relationship that man and God had in that primordial state of consciousness called Eden.

"The fear of the Lord is the beginning of wisdom: and the knowledge of the holy is understanding. For by me thy days shall be multiplied, and the years of thy life shall be increased." – Proverbs 9:10-11 KJV

For so long, man has been ignorant of the fact that he is truly a temple in which God dwells. This lack of knowledge has caused man to perish without fully living the life he was created to live. As man begins to fear God or begins to give praise and reverence to the Creator within, he will no longer look to the world without for the solution to his problems, but will begin his journey within. Through the practice of frequent prayer and meditation with thanksgiving, man will begin to witness an outpouring of peace and tranquility within his heart and mind that will surpasses all understanding. This peace is the result of continuing to remove the blockage (carnal thoughts) between the mind of God (Eden) and the mind of man (Pishon), which prevented man from living the life he was created to live.

Havilah: Where Gold Resides

"The name of the first is Pishon: that is it which compassed the whole land of Havilah, where there is gold; And the gold of that land is good: there is bdellium and the onyx stone." — Genesis 2:11-12 KJV

Throughout history, when man has gained knowledge to the possible location of gold, his instincts has driven him to acquire more knowledge as to the definite coordinates of this location. After putting this knowledge to the test, he may initially find that the calculated coordinates are incorrect, and with much willpower he continues the search to find the correct coordinates. However, with the passage of time, he begins to discover gold shavings, which assures him of being close to the true location of the gold. This reassurance of possibly striking gold has equipped him with a better understanding of how to proceed further with the gold mining process. As he continues to discover more gold shavings and small nuggets of gold, his prior understandings reconstruct themselves into self-evident truths to fuel him to acquire greater truths about the gold buried deep beneath the Earth.

After a duration of time, man finds himself being solely delighted in just the pure search for gold. He has found comfort in knowing that within the depths of the Earth dwells an indefinite amount of gold. For it is only when he turns to look at his gold fortune, he realizes the riches acquired are more than he could have ever dreamed of; and the acquisition of more gold is solely dependent upon his willpower to obtain more.

Within the Bible, and many other religious texts, gold is representative of wisdom. The acquisition of wisdom is obtained through a process governed by Mental Universal Laws that gives wisdom to all men liberally. The ability to allow the waters (knowledge) to flow freely from Eden (Creative Mind) into the river Pishon (the mind of man) can be likened unto man's search for gold. But to merely have knowledge of the means to obtaining wisdom is not enough. For the enlightened man knows that Christ is the power and wisdom that lives within him.

"But unto them which are called both Jews and Greeks, Christ the power of God, and the wisdom of God." – 1 Corinthians 1:24 KJV

Man must put this knowledge to the test and begin to seek a greater understanding of Christ's wisdom within.

"Examine yourselves to see whether you are still in the Christian faith. Test yourselves! Don't you recognize that you are people in whom Jesus Christ lives? Could it be that you're failing the test?" – 2 Corinthians 13:5 KJV

When man seeks a greater understanding of God (Creative Mind) he is allowing the waters of Eden to flow into Pishon (mind of man), thus removing stones (materialistic thoughts) and polishing the precious treasures of beryllium and onyx through the process of weathering. The weathering process of man can be likened to the life experiences he undergoes that test his ability to withstand life's fiery trials. If man survives the tests of his trials, he will surely come out as pure gold.

The gold (wisdom) hidden within the land of Havilah will be reached once the waters of the Pishon River take shape into a constant and free flowing cleansing source having the ability to erode the land of Havilah and give access to the gold (wisdom) within.

"My brethren, count it all joy when ye fall into divers temptations; Knowing this, that the trying of your faith worketh patience. But let patience have her perfect work, that ye may be perfect and entire, wanting nothing. If any of you lack wisdom, let him ask of God, that giveth to all men liberally, and upbraideth not; and it shall be given him." – James 1:2-5 KJV

Fig Tree Tool

If one's desire is to develop that "thing", that "It-Factorness" or uniqueness of quality about himself, he must not look to the world without for solutions, but must turn inwards and begin the mining process for his divine treasures of uniqueness. These hidden treasures are the laboratory contents that allow him to perform his own mental alchemy in the laboratory within. If he can persist in the feeling of already having accomplished that which he desires, he will soon see the fruits of his labor bear witness in his world without. For if he is attentive, he will notice that his innermost desires will begin putting forth leaves to indicate that the reaping time is near.

"Now learn a parable of the fig tree; When his branch is yet tender, and putteth forth leaves, ye know that the summer is nigh: So likewise ye, when ye shall see all these things, know that it is near, even at the doors. Verily I say unto you, This generation shall not pass, till

Do You Know the Parable?

all these things be fulfilled. Heaven and earth shall pass away, but my words shall not pass away." – Matthew 25:32-35 KJV

CHAPTER FIVE

Have You Found Him?

"Philip findeth Nathanael, and saith unto him, We have found him, of whom Moses in the law, and the prophets, did write, Jesus of Nazareth, the son of Joseph." – John 1:45 KJV

"Nathanael said unto him, whence knowest thou me? Jesus answered and said unto him, Before that Philip called thee, when thou wast under the fig tree, I saw thee." – John 1:48 KJV

The World

A man can be both living and dead at the same time. When I say "dead," I mean that the spiritual part of the man is still asleep, and has not yet awakened to the power that lies within him. For a man can be walking around, breathing, and have his outer bodily functions working—even though his spiritual self is not alive, or has not yet awakened.

One will never read a passage of scripture in the Book of Genesis in which Adam wakes from his deep spiritual sleep; for the first human Adam represents man's early evolutionary state of consciousness, where he is only aware of his body consciousness, and not fully aware of the Orchestrating One that truly allows him to move and have his being. The second man Adam, which is the Jesus Christ of us, is representative of the being that dwells within him, through him, and through all animate and inanimate creations.

"But now is Christ risen from the dead, and become the first fruits of them that slept. For as in Adam all die, even so in Christ shall all be made alive." – 2 Corinthians 15:20-22 KJV

The True Definition of Sin

Ever since I was a child, I have been curious about the definition and meaning of words and phrases. However, there was one word that I had never gotten around to looking up in my early life. I guess I had assumed the definition was obvious from having gone to church every Monday through Saturday, and twice on Sunday. This word, when stated to others or me, gave me the sense that the recipient of the word was the scum of the Earth, or that he was some filthy substance that resided at the bottom of trash barrels. However, thanks to my high school Spanish classes and other etymological book sources in my later life, I have learned the true meaning of the word "sin."

In Latin, the word "sin" means without, which is the opposite of within. Other meanings of the word *sin* include separated from, missing the mark, or lacking. When man grasps hold of the true definition of the word *sin*, he will not only begin to understand the true meaning behind the Biblical scriptures, but he will also begin to unveil the spiritual meaning behind other religious "isms" around the world as well.

"I said therefore unto you, that ye shall die in your sins; for if ye believe not that I AM he, ye shall die in your sins." – John 8:24 KJV

Where To Find Him?

Man, when in his early evolutionary state of consciousness, believes in a god outside of himself and searches aimlessly in the vast world *without* for a god to save him from his sins (separation). In worshipping a god outside of himself, he has unknowingly set himself up for idol worship, or for the worship of some false and illusionary form of God. In man's sinful (separated) state, he does not yet realize that God (I AM) does not reside in the earthquake or in the fire, but in that still, small voice *within*.

"Be still, and know that I AM God..." – Psalm 46:10 KJV

The location of God (I AM) is stated numerous times within the Bible, but man, with the veil of carnality still covering his face, cannot see past the words of the Bible to detect the spiritual meaning behind it. The spiritual awakening of man begins once he starts his journey inward and becomes one with the life-giving spirit that lies within.

"But their minds were blinded: for until this day remaineth the same vail untaken away in the reading of the old testament; which vail is done away in Christ. But even unto this day, when Moses is read, the vail is upon their heart. Nevertheless when it shall turn to the Lord, the veil shall be taken away." – 2 Corinthians 3:14-16 KJV

Man's journey inward will lead him to the realm of infinite treasures, where the "one Moses in law and the prophets did write" resides. Man's journey inward will lead him to that spiritual locale where the streets are paved with gold (wisdom) and the angels sing "Holy, Holy, Holy." This spiritual location is what the Bible calls the "Kingdom of Heaven" or the "Kingdom of God (I AM)".

The Kingdom of Heaven

"I said therefore unto you, that ye shall die in your sins; for if ye believe not that I AM he, ye shall die in your sins." – John 8:24 KJV

One of the most debated topics of all time, within both the religious sects and various "isms" of the world, is the location of the place called Heaven, or the Kingdom of God. Man perishes for a lack of knowledge, and it is his lack of knowledge of the whereabouts his I-AMness that is the main cause of sin (separation) from his true inner source of power and freedom. The carnal-minded man has eyes, but cannot see (discern); and has ears but cannot hear (understand). Man, in his unenlightened state of consciousness, is therefore ever learning, but never able to come to the knowledge of the truth.

Man's lacking of the knowledge of spiritual things is a result of his ignorance of the spiritual concepts hidden behind the veil of carnality. He also plunges himself into deeper states of ignorance when he tries to fill the spiritual voids by looking to the outer world for self-proclaimed wise men, gurus, and sages to answer questions concerning the purpose for his life. However, it is these self-proclaimed wise men, gurus, and sages of the world who continue to teach their flock of sheep to believe in a god outside of themselves, but never teaching them of the Jesus Christ (I AM) that lives within them. Therefore, it is a prime case of the "blind leading the blind."

"Examine yourselves to see whether you are still in the Christian faith. Test yourselves! Don't you recognize that you are people in whom Jesus Christ lives? Could it be that you're failing the test?" – 2 Corinthians 13:5 GW

"Don't you know that you are God's temple and that God's Spirit lives in you?" – 1 Corinthians 3:16 GW

Fig Tree Tool

When man comes to fully realize that the same Spirit that raised Jesus from the dead dwells within him too, he will then realize that the power to change the circumstances of his life resides within his control as well. The acquisition of this truth equips man with the a greater understanding of freewill. Man has the freewill to plant whatever seeds (thoughts) within the garden of his mind that represent his true desires; and in due season will reap a harvest matching his desires. To find this Universal Power is to grasp hold of the reaping and sowing power that Moses in the law, and the prophets, did write about.

"But seek ye first the kingdom of God, and his righteousness; and all these things shall be added unto you."—Matthew 6:33 KJV

However, to seek this Universal Power outwardly, like the carnal minded (Gentiles) man, is to seek in vain.

Do You Know the Parable?

But when the spiritually minded (Jew) man first seeks within, accompanied with righteousness (right-thinking), he will be granted all the desires of his heart.

"For he is not a Jew, which one outwardly; neither is that circumcision, which is outward in the flesh; But he is a Jew, which is one inwardly; and circumcision is that of the heart, in the spirit, and not in the letter; whose praise is not of men, but of God." — Romans 2:28-29 KJV

CHAPTER SIX

The Journey to Almondiblathaim

"And they departed from Oboth, and pitched in Ijeabarim, in the border of Moab. And they departed from Ijeabarim, and pitched in Dibongad. And they removed from Dibongad, and encamped in Almondiblathaim." – Numbers 33:44-46 KJV

The Israelites' Journey through the Wilderness

The Bible, as well as many other religious documents, gives details of how Moses led the Hebrews out of the land of Egypt and journeyed with them to the Promised Land. The goal of Moses was to lead the Israelites to this paradise of sustenance that flowed with milk and honey. However, the journey of the Hebrew people wasn't always a pleasant one. The Israelites encountered many trials and tribulations that tested their physical, mental, and spiritual endurance. They were repeatedly persecuted and attacked by other tribes in the various regions. The Book of Numbers 33:1-46 summarizes the 40-year journey of the Israelites out of the land of Egypt and through the wilderness. The Israelites encamped at a total of 42 different locations while journeying through the wilderness. Of the 42 locations, the 40th locale — *Almondiblathaim* — is a very significant one, because it was the last place of encampment before they were able to *look* over into the Promised Land.

Have you ever heard of *Almondiblathaim*? If you read about the journey of the Israelites out of the land of Egypt, you will find that Almondiblathaim is the last place of encampment before Moses was able to look over into the Promise Land. The word

"Almondiblathaim" means "the hiding of two fig cakes." After encamping in Almondiblathaim, Moses went up to the highest peak of the Abraim Mountains to look out over to *see* the Promised Land. It was at Abraim that Moses died.

After leaving Abraim, the Israelites then went into Abelshittim, and abided in the meadows of the acacias.

Out of the Darkness and into the Marvelous Light

As I have already noted, the Bible is, by far, the greatest psychological book ever written. The carnal-minded man, when in his unveiled state of consciousness, cannot understand the Biblical scriptures due to his inability to discern spiritual matters. The truths contained within the Scriptures are like strong wine to the earthly-minded man; they cause him to fall asleep or become frustrated while reading the Bible. The natural man, thus, cannot comprehend the spiritual things of God; and neither can he know them, because they can only be discerned spiritually. The carnal man's unveiled state of consciousness is so interwoven with much religious dogma and worldly thinking. It is the veil of carnality that prevents the unenlightened man from seeing the spiritual underpinnings of all things. When man begins to awake to the Christ within him, he will experience an increasing ability to discern the spiritual meanings of the Bible; his purpose in life, and obtain a greater knowledge about the inner workings of his own mind.

The Israelites' journey out of Egypt and through the 42 encampments of the wilderness is a beautifully detailed illustration of man's journey to enlightenment and his passage from darkness to light.

The Journey Out of Egypt

The word "Egypt" is derived from the Hebrew name Mizraim, which means misery, bondage, tribulation, shut-in, and restraint. Hence the phrase, "Misery (Mizery) loves company". In the Biblical story, Egypt is the country where the Hebrew people were held in bondage for a number of years as slaves. However, from a spiritual perspective, Egypt represents a darkened state of conscious within the realm and inner workings of the body conscious.

Before I go any further, let me clearly state that a full awareness of the body conscious is necessary in the conquest to master the whole man; which is made up of body, mind, and spirit. That is why some of the most prominent spiritual leaders in the Bible started their early lives in Egypt and progressed their way up towards higher spiritual awareness. While man is in his unregenerate, Egyptian state of consciousness, he doesn't yet realize his spiritual connection to the universe, nature, and other people. This lack of spiritual knowledge leaves him with a feeling of helplessness, as if he was a small pawn on the grand stage of the universe. The goal of the spiritual man, which is buried deep within the soul, is to regain his spiritual birthright and lead the whole man into the path of righteousness.

The Awakening Process

The true definition of repentance is to undergo a radical change of mind from a former belief of error to a belief in the truth. When man repents from his sin (separated) state of consciousness, he undergoes a radical change of mind from a former belief in a god outside of himself, to the realization that God (I AM) is within or truly at hand.

"In those days came John the Baptist, preaching in the wilderness of Judaea, And saying, Repent ye: for the kingdom of heaven is at hand." – Matthew 3:1-2 KJV

Before the whole man can move into a higher spiritual realization of himself, he must first awaken from the sleep (bondage) in which he believes that his mortal body is all he is made of. The journey to Almondiblathaim, or the journey within, embarks with an initial cleansing or washing away (Red Sea) of former carnal beliefs such as religious dogmas (the Pharaoh's army) that have kept man in a sort of mental bondage. The religious dogmas mentioned here are likened to the Biblical pharisaical traditions that taught and preached about a god separate (sin) from man.

"And when he was demanded of the Pharisees, when the kingdom of God should come, he answered them and said, The kingdom of God cometh not with observation: Neither shall they say, Lo here! Or, lo there! for, behold, the kingdom of God is within you."
– Luke 17:20-21 KJV

"Examine yourselves to see whether you are still in the Christian faith. Test yourselves! Don't you recognize that you are people in whom Jesus Christ lives? Could it be that you're failing the test?" – 2 Corinthians 13:5 GW

Once the repentance and cleansing process have taken place within the mind of man, he must begin the process of re-learning who he really is. This process embarks man on a journey through a number of conscious states in which he must conquer. The pilgrimages through the wilderness are the encampments where man must retrain the undisciplined mind with valuable lessons of Truth that will bring his body, mind, and spirit into one harmonious state. The conquering of each state is solely dependent upon his ability to trust his inner spiritual I-AMness for guidance. Overcoming of the trials and tribulations within each conscious state is instrumental in developing man's relationship with his inner I-AMness by teaching him to trust spirit rather than on his carnal abilities. Once man has conquered the various states of temptation within the wilderness of mind, he will then have acquired the ability and willpower to enter into his last place of encampment—his Almondiblathaim.

"And another of his disciples said unto him, Lord, suffer me first to go and bury my father. But Jesus said unto him, Follow me; and let the dead bury the dead. And when he was entered into a ship, his disciples followed him." – Matthew 8:21-23 KJV

When man has centralized all his forces inward, he is allowing the remaining of his carnal thinking patterns to die and begin to follow the higher spiritual thoughts of his I-AMness; allowing him to focus on the vision of the new spiritual state of consciousness, the Promised Land.

Abiding in Almondiblathaim

"He that dwelleth in the secret place of the most High shall abide under the shadow of the Almighty. I will say of the Lord, He is my refuge and my fortress." – Psalm 91:1-2 KJV

When man abides in Almondiblathaim or within, he is dwelling in the secret place of the Most High. While in Almondiblathaim (holy ground), he is able to look over into Canaan (the Promise Land) and begin to see the vision or the higher ideal of himself. Since he is now on Holy Ground, he must take off his shoes (carnal understanding), and learn from the Master by sitting at the feet of his I-AMness. By focusing on his I-AMness through the medium of prayer, meditation, and thanksgiving, he will receive influxes of the light (wisdom) and love to guide him into the Promised Land, or higher ideal of himself.

"There is no fear in love; but perfect love casteth out fear; because fear hath torment. He that feareth is not made perfect in love." – 1 John 4:18 KJV

"For this corruptible must put on incorruption, and this mortal must put on immortality. So when this corruptible shall have put on incorruption, and this mortal shall have put on immortality, then shall be brought to pass the saying that is written, Death is swallowed up in victory." – 1 Corinthians 15:53-54 KJV

Fig Tree Tool

There are so many hurting people in the world. These hurting people are composed of individuals that society may even call rich, poor, educated, uneducated, gifted, ungifted, sick, well, black, white, young, or old. Notwithstanding of who, or what, these hurting people may feel themselves to be, or how society may label them, each individual must come to terms with the one universal truth, that: In order to find healing, peace, joy, and bliss, the individual must turn away from the world without and realize that true happiness is only found by turning to heaven (within.)

"If my people, which are called by my name, shall humble themselves, and pray, and seek my face, and turn from their wicked ways; then will I hear from Heaven, and will forgive their sin, and will heal their land." – 2 Chronicles 7:14 KJV

When a man turns from the world of Pharaoh (without) and begins his journey towards the doors of Almondiblathaim (within), he will begin to understand the lesson of the fig tree, and the fruits of his labor will bear witness to his new state of consciousness.

"Now learn a parable of the fig tree; When his branch is yet tender, and putteth forth leaves, ye know that summer is nigh: So likewise ye, when ye shall see all these things, know that it is near, even at the doors." – Matthew 24:32-33 KJV

CHAPTER SEVEN

The Seventh Day: The Art of Silent Meditation

"Be still, and know that I AM God..." Psalm 46:10 KJV

Silent Meditation

One of the best pieces of advice I can give to the spiritual truth seeker is to not only work hard at developing a healthy prayer life, but to also develop the habit of performing daily and silent meditation. As far back as I can remember, my mother taught my siblings and I the importance of making one's requests known to God through prayer and supplication with thanksgiving. Now, even unto this day, I pray daily and am careful to give thanks afterwards. The ceremony of praise and thanksgiving can be likened to a production containing all the sustenance necessary for bringing your unseen requests into their seen and crystalized forms. For whatever you praise and give thanksgiving towards, that is what will increase in your life.

I learned later in life that it is through the medium of silent mediation that the womb of creation, or the womb of the subconscious mind, takes in those "production-line" substances and brings form to each and every prayer request. Over the years, through hard work and persistence, I have added the art of silent meditation to my daily practice. However, I must be completely honest in saying that when the distractions of life arise, I too must alter my meditation schedule as necessary, sometimes even shortening my meditation periods. Nevertheless, the race for spiritual growth and improvement goes not to the swift or the strong, but to the one who endures to the end. That is why it is so important to strive for a daily regimen where silent meditation is involved. As I write this message, I am currently able to integrate at least two hours of daily meditation into my daily routine, comprised of one hour of meditation in the morning and one hour of meditation at night.

After much verbiage about the importance of silent meditation, the aspiring meditative practitioner may be asking one of the most important questions related to silent meditation. This leads me to reminisce about the moment I was asked the question most common amongst aspiring truth seekers. This particular individual was interested in seeking the true nature of himself by integrating meditation into his daily life. After approaching me, he asked the simple, but very important question: "Stacey, what do you think about when you meditate?"

My reply was simply, "Nothing."

Into the Holy Chamber of "No-Thing-ness"

"For God speaketh once, yea twice, yet man perceiveth it not. In a dream, in a vision of the night, when deep sleep falleth upon men, in slumberings upon the bed; Then he opened the ears of men, and sealed their instruction, That he may withdraw man from his purpose, and hid pride from man." - Job 33:14-17 KJV

"Through faith we understand that the worlds were framed by the word of God, so that things which are seen were not made of things which do appear." - Hebrews 11:2-3 KJV

While in the realm of deep meditation or deep sleep, the carnal mind becomes paralyzed, and the subconscious mind is able to receive uninhibited impressions or instructions from the conscious mind. It is within the formless deepness of ourselves that our

Do You Know the Parable?

I-AMness receives instructions about our innermost desires, and instructs the whole man as to how to bring forth our desires. The subconscious mind can be likened to a beloved wife who is eternally faithful to bringing forth from her womb whatever seeds of impression her husband (consciousness) impregnates her with, and producing a direct replica of the seed (thought) which has been sown.

"It was but a little that I passed from them, but I passed from them, but I found him whom my soul loveth: I held him, and would not let him go, until I had brought him into my mother's house, and into the chamber of her that conceived me." - Song of Solomon 3:4 KJV

This is why it is of so much importance not to bring ANY undesirable thoughts into the holy chambers of matrimony, but to bring only those things you wish to manifest in your world without. So many people go into meditation or into sleep with so many unpleasant thoughts about themselves, and wonder why their lives are in such disarray. After the act of thinking or creating that mental image or vision of your ideal self, one should rest during the appointed interval of time (Sabbath); knowing that the ideal, or vision , of oneself is good and will surely come to pass.

Keeping the Sabbath Holy

"And on the seventh day God ended his work which he had made; and he rested on the seventh day from all his work which he had made. And God blessed the seventh day, and sanctified it: because that in it he had rested from all his work which God created and made." - Genesis 2:2-3 KJV

The carnal minded man, with his limited perception, oftentimes only perceives that which his senses dictate to be true. His limited perception is mainly due to his lack of spiritual awareness and his inability to adhere to the Laws of Cause and Effect, which are the governing force behind all things. When the unenlightened man turns his understanding of the laws into applied truths, he will in turn create a better world for himself to live in. For with obtaining these truths, the enlightened man will be able to testify that all things—whether in the form of houses, skyscrapers, poems, businesses, or events—first started with a strong, underlying belief (faith) in a thought (word) before any such things were manifested.

"Through faith we understand that the worlds were framed by the word of God, so that things which are seen were not made of things which do appear." John 1:3 KJV

Man is always thinking (creating). Therefore, the spiritually awakened man is careful to only think (create) and meditate on things that will bring him joy, peace and bliss. Once the duration of the creative process is complete, the enlightened man knows the importance of resting on the Sabbath day and allowing his inner I-AMness to bring form to his innermost desires in his world without.

When man keeps the Sabbath Day holy, he is making a dedicated effort to refrain from thinking (creating) anything that might negatively impact his creation. He must know within himself that his creation is wholly good, beautiful, and wonderfully made. He should not ponder over or question himself or his creation, but to only "Let Go and Let God," by allowing the connection between his inner I-AMness and the I-AMness within every other living thing to peacefully work in concert. In due time, man will witness the bringing forth of his innermost desires onto the "movie screen" of space in his world without. Therefore, his righteousness (right-thinking) is crucial in bringing forth his manifestations in the exact image and likeness of the original thought seeds or words planted within.

"But seek ye first the kingdom of God, and his righteousness; and all these things shall be added unto you. Take therefore no thought for the morrow: for the morrow shall take thought for the things of itself. Sufficient unto the day is the evil thereof." - Matthew 6:33-34 KJV

Tell No Man and Seek No Counsel

Many times in life, after man has believed, planned, and allowed the spirit to move him into the execution of his vision, he encounters many obstacles. Most perceived obstacles are in the form of "red tape", such as roadblocks and perceived trials that seem to set him back from obtaining his goals. However, the toughest obstacles to overcome may sometimes come from negative feedback from other people. As an emotional being, it can be hard for even the most spiritually minded individual to be unaffected by adverse words from friends, family and the like. But nevertheless, it must be kept in mind that no one can counsel you about the UNIQUE ideas you have. However, take care, this cannot be confused with the resources (books, professionals, etc.) that will be drawn into your life to assist you in the fulfillment of your vision. These resources will automatically be drawn into your life by the inner workings of the great I AM.

This is why it's important to tell no one of your innermost desires, and to let the fruits you bear speak for you. Let it be a secret between you and your inner I-AMness. The telling of no man allows two things to happen; it allows you to:

(1) not be set back with unrighteous (wrong-thinking) counsel; and

(2) to organically add fuel onto an ever-increasing fire(desire) that can only be quenched by the full manifestation of your creation.

Do You Know the Parable?

The welling up of the desire within is the fuel needed for the mind to maintain a watchful eye, until the thing hoped for comes to past. Therefore, put yourself on your watchtower, sit back, grab some popcorn, and allow the I AM's film projector within to shine light upon the picture screen of space. Watch with an attitude of discernment at how all things visible, invisible, animate, and inanimate fall in line and play their part in concert to bring forth your innermost desire.

The repetition of experiencing events and people divinely fall into place, and provides the necessary iterations to build you up on your most holy faith. So I encourage you, the reader, to endure to the end. If your vision seems to tarry or not come fast enough, I encourage you to deny any wicked (negative) thoughts and hold fast, knowing that your vision has an appointed time for manifestation, and will not be late.

"I will stand upon my watch, and set me upon the tower, and will watch to see what he will say unto me, and what I shall answer when I am reproved. And the Lord answered me, and said, Write the vision, and make it plain upon tables, that he may run that readeth it. For the vision is yet for an appointed time, but at the end it shall speak, and not lie: though it tarry, wait for it; because it will surely come, it will not tarry." - Habakkuk 2:1-3 KJV

Even if it is not yet seen with the natural eye, go ahead and begin praising and thanking God (I AM) for your blessing (manifestation) right now. You do not have to wait until the battle is over; you can claim the victory and shout it out now.

Fig Tree Tool

"O my God, my soul is cast down within me: therefore will I remember thee from the land of Jordan, and of the Hermonites, from the hill Mizar. Deep calleth unto deep at the noise of thy waterspouts: all thy waves and thy billows are gone over me." - Psalms 42:6-7 KJV

The way you see yourself, the way others view you, and the things, events, and people you draw into your life are directly proportional to how you TRULY feel within the vast deepness of yourself. Your magnetism or drawing power flows from the depths of your being (I-AMness), and attracts into your life that which you TRULY feel yourself to be. Therefore, if you want to change the circumstances of your life, do not concern yourself with trying to change the world or others. Though it may sound cliché or like a line from a motivational speech; the truth of the matter is that the power for change ultimately resides within you.

I encourage you, the reader, to take time each day to practice silent meditation. Know what you want; see yourself becoming whom you desire to be until the feeling of accomplishment flows through your entire body. Then go into the silent meditation, and rest in the assurance that the I-AMness within you and the I-AMness within everything in the universe is working in concert to bring your desires into full fruition.

<u>Do You Know the Parable?</u>

ABOUT THE AUTHOR

Stacey L. Mizell, Sr. is an ordained minister who enjoys reading the Bible, meditating, walking, boxing, and spending time with his family and friends. He is the founder of Fig Tree Tools™, an organization dedicated to promoting Universal Oneness. Through writing and lecturing in various cities in the United States, the aim of Fig Tree Tools™ is to teach individuals how to become more aware of their inner spirituality, as well as to develop a greater awareness of the spirituality within others.

In 2002, Stacey received his Bachelor of Science degree in Industrial and Systems Engineering from the Georgia Institute of Technology. In 2008, he received his Masters Degree in Accounting and Financial Management from the Keller Graduate School of DeVry.

Do You Know the Parable?

As for as any degrees in divinity or religion, he has none. His ability to interpret the underlying meanings of Biblical scriptures has come directly through the medium of divine revelation.

"And he said unto them, this kind can come forth by nothing, but by prayer and fasting."
— Mark 9:29 KJV

Fig Tree Tools™ Online

Your Internet gateway to a virtual environment for obtaining inspiring and spiritually enlightening books, articles and information from Fig Tree Tools™.

Fig Tree Tools™ Online is located at
www.figtreetools.com

FIG TREE TOOL NEWS

Every month you'll receive updated information about our upcoming books and any new features that have been added to our site. We do this to keep you well informed about any of our new books, articles or information that may aid you in your spiritual growth.

Do You Know the Parable?

Subscribe to Fig Tree Tools News at:
www.figtreetools.com/newsletters

www.ingramcontent.com/pod-product-compliance
Lightning Source LLC
LaVergne TN
LVHW091315080426
835510LV00007B/507